Retirement

David Winter

GW00702921

BIBLE READINGS FOR SPECIAL TIMES

...for those times when we want to hear God's word speaking to us clearly

Retirement

David Winter

Text copyright © David Winter 2005
The author asserts the moral right
to be identified as the author of this work

Published by
The Bible Reading Fellowship
First Floor, Elsfield Hall
15–17 Elsfield Way, Oxford OX2 8FG

ISBN 1 84101 430 3
First published 2005
10 9 8 7 6 5 4 3 2 1 0
All rights reserved

Acknowledgments
Scripture quotations are taken from The New Revised Standard Version of
the Bible, Anglicized Edition, copyright © 1989, 1995 by the Division of
Christian Education of the National Council of the Churches of Christ in the
United States of America, and are used by permission. All rights reserved.

A catalogue record for this book is available from the British Library

Printed by Gutenberg Press, Tarxien, Malta

Introduction

It is, of course, a life of bliss. One can get up when one likes, slob around half the morning in a dressing-gown, drift into town for a coffee and a bit of shopping, potter in the garden, watch cricket on the television without feeling guilty, and play a leisurely mid-week round of golf on a half-deserted course. The female counterpart, of course, may offer a different catalogue, but in the same vein. Retirement? I can't wait for it.

Or, of course, it's not a bit like that. You foolishly thought that retirement would mean acres of time to explore every avenue of leisure, every byway of delight. All those things for which there was once no time would now be beckoning. In the event, what has happened is that you find you've taken on a garden too large for you to manage; or arthritis or angina have wrecked your golf handicap; or the wretched vicar has talked you into being church warden and a governor of the local church school. Not only that, but all of a sudden—having no longer any decent excuse to put it off—you find yourself visiting all the friends and relatives whom you stupidly promised you'd visit when you retired. The diary is as full as ever, and you now know exactly why people who were already retired made that silly joke about not being able to imagine how they ever had time to fit in work.

For the Christian, earthly life begins at birth and ends at death. Everything in between is part of that precious gift of God, and we know that that inevitably includes the process of growing up, the experiences of youth and middle age, and then of advancing years. In each phase of life there are potential joys and potential sorrows and disappointments, and it is unrealistic to pretend that the process of ageing is entirely a welcome one. On the other hand, just as adolescence has its heartaches and tears, so it also has its highlights and fun, and growing old (unbelievable as it may seem to the young) also has its profound joys. On the whole, the older people I know are not marked by universal misery and grumpiness: we are not all Victor Meldrews! For many, the evening hours of life are deeply satisfying, and all the more so when they are seen as part of that one precious gift of life.

This book of readings from the Bible is about 'retirement', even though the very notion would have been completely baffling to people of biblical times. There were then, of course, no pension schemes, no retirement homes, no 'sheltered accommodation'—and certainly no legal age at which you were permitted, or even expected, to stop work.

Nevertheless, people grew old, slowly lost their physical vigour and strength, and became more dependent on others—in their case, the extended family, which willingly accepted the responsibility of caring for its senior members. The Bible addresses their situation, as well as seeing life whole. It speaks of the problems of change, of the passing of time, of the value of family life, of a creation that 'wears out like a garment' (Psalm 102:26). But it sets all of this within one utter certainty, and that is the reliability and changelessness of the Creator. If this little book is to be of any help to those who are facing what we call 'retirement' (or are already in it), it will only be because of that transcending truth: 'You are the same, and your years have no end' (Psalm 102:27).

PSALM 139:13–16 (NRSV, ABRIDGED)

Fearfully and wonderfully made

For it was you who formed my inward parts; you knit me together in my mother's womb. I praise you, for I am fearfully and wonderfully made. Wonderful are your works; that I know very well. My frame was not hidden from you, when I was being made in secret, intricately woven in the depths of the earth… In your book were written all the days that were formed for me, when none of them as yet existed.

We all have a beginning, and these verses place its minutest details in the purposes of God. From the moment of conception, when our cells begin to multiply, embarking on the amazing process that eventually shapes a tiny human person, the Creator is involved.

The ancient world knew little about those pre-natal developments, but today's parents-to-be can follow the unborn child's progress through scans, tests and foetal monitors. Yet still there is an element of the miraculous to the whole process, so that even hardened health professionals speak of it with respect and, on occasions, awe. That is certainly the reaction of the young parents watching on a screen the child they will one day hold in their arms. I remember one young father saying that he had never been sure about belief in God until he witnessed the birth of his first child. Truly, 'I am fearfully and wonderfully made'.

It seems appropriate to begin a book of readings on retirement by going right back to the beginning. The point the psalmist is making, of course, is that all of my life, from its very beginning in the womb until the moment of death, is the gift of God. I could not give myself life. I could not shape my own limbs, organs or brain. Everything I am is gift, and has been from the very beginning.

The God who formed me in the womb is still able to work in my life, 'fearfully and wonderfully'.

GENESIS 12:1–2, 4 (NRSV, ABRIDGED)

Days of change

Now the Lord said to Abram, 'Go from your country and your kindred and your father's house to the land that I will show you. I will make of you a great nation, and I will bless you, and make your name great, so that you will be a blessing… So Abram went, as the Lord had told him… Abram was seventy-five years old when he departed from Haran.

Here is one of the great moments of biblical history. Abram (well past modern retirement age, we note) is a God-fearing resident of the city of Ur, in the land we would now call Iraq. He feels urged by God to leave his home and travel west, taking his whole household with him. By any standards, it was a massive leap of faith.

Yet if Abram had *not* gone, if he had reckoned that at his age he was entitled to a quiet life, the biblical story would never even have begun. That single traumatic step of change was a key that opened a new life, yet to be rich with promise, meaning and purpose.

We live now in an age when change is taken for granted—'portfolio employment' rather than a 'job for life', 'relocation' as a common experience. Yet, even in an age of change, retirement does loom across the horizon as a major junction: all change here. Quite suddenly, fixed points in our routine alter: no train to catch, no hours to keep, no deadlines to meet. On the other hand, there is probably time for things we have longed to do. Change may be daunting in prospect, but at least it opens up possibilities.

For Abram, it brought an utterly new revelation of the God he had trusted but knew only hazily. For the human race, because of him, it brought eventually the most precious revelation of all, in the birth of Jesus, son of Abram, Son of God

To stay where we are and do nothing is always an option, but often the wrong one!

ACTS 6:5–6, 8 (NRSV)

A new role

They chose Stephen, a man full of faith and the Holy Spirit,
together with Philip, Prochorus, Nicanor, Timon, Parmenas,
and Nicolaus, a proselyte of Antioch. They had these men
stand before the apostles, who prayed and laid their hands
on them... Stephen, full of grace and power, did great
wonders and signs among the people.

Here we have a different kind of change: not of location, like Abram's, but of role. This is an instance of the kind of change many people experience in retirement.

Our reading gives us a fascinating glimpse into the life of the earliest Christian Church. The believers still ate their meals together, but by now they numbered several thousand and the twelve apostles could no longer be expected to administer the daily distribution of food. Instead, seven trustworthy men were chosen to supervise it. Among them was Stephen, who immediately responded to the call by showing great spiritual gifts and wisdom.

He was soon ministering far beyond the matter of food distribution. He did 'great wonders and signs' (v. 8) and showed eloquence and wisdom in putting across the Christian case.

Retirement sometimes uncovers great spiritual gifts and calling, into ministry, for example. I know of people who have discovered a talent for banner making, music, or administration. Like Stephen, they may have expected to do a simple menial job but found that in the process all kinds of hidden gifts were released.

One of the biggest mistakes we can make approaching retirement is to think that 'effective' life is over. History is full of people whose major achievements began after they had passed the legendary three score years and ten.

'Grow old along with me, the best is yet to be...' (Robert Browning)

LUKE 1:12–15a (NRSV, ABRIDGED)

Never too late

When Zechariah saw [the angel]… fear overwhelmed him.
But the angel said to him, 'Do not be afraid, Zechariah, for
your prayer has been heard. Your wife Elizabeth will bear you
a son… You will have joy and gladness, and many will rejoice
at his birth, for he will be great in the sight of the Lord.'

Infertility was a terrible affliction in a culture where children were needed to inherit the land and care for their parents in their old age. The elderly priest Zechariah and his wife were childless and well past child-bearing age. So when he had this vision, he must have wondered what it meant. Was their life's wish and prayer finally to be granted? Or was the vision itself a self-induced delusion?

Two common emotions lie behind his reaction: the feeling that it's 'too good to be true'and the fear that it's all too late. When good things happen late in life, both these feelings can emerge.

Zechariah gives the lie to both. Old as he and his wife were, a great joy and fulfilment was to be theirs: not just a son, but one who would be 'great in the sight of the Lord'.

In post-retirement life, we may feel that we can no longer expect good things—from now on it's downhill all the way! Of course, as we get older, bodies and minds show signs of ageing. Yet I think that very few people who are experiencing them would regard the post-retirement years as a relentless process of decline.

We may make new discoveries. Many people have come late to prayer, for instance, or to the joy of a regular retreat. Within the family, advancing age often deepens rather than weakens our ties with loved ones. For such things, it is never 'too late'.

Zechariah and Elizabeth may have felt that nothing significant would ever occur in their remaining years. In the providence of God, however, the most important event of their lives lay just nine months ahead.

LUKE 2:36–38 (NRSV, ABRIDGED)

Faithful to the last

There was also a prophet, Anna the daughter of Phanuel, of the tribe of Asher. She was of a great age… She never left the temple but worshipped there with fasting and prayer night and day. At that moment she came, and began to praise God and to speak about the child to all who were looking for the redemption of Jerusalem.

Anna, and also the elderly Simeon, who kept watch in the temple for the coming of the Messiah, are wonderful examples of faithfulness. Both were old, yet still hoped to see God's blessing on his people. They represent 'faithful Israel', those who had not been led astray either by Gentile ways or by the empty legalism of the scribes and Pharisees.

Happily, many churches are full of such people, who have led long and often hard lives, and for whom in old age a marvellously serene faith has emerged. It is as though, like Simeon and Anna, they retain a living hope of God's blessing. Often they are the 'good neighbours' in their streets or villages, happy to mind someone's cat or look after their key when they're away, and always with a smile and words of encouragement. Old age also has its full quota of moaners, of course, and most churches have a few of those as well! But often it is the 'faithful remnant' that sets the tone of a church.

Simeon and Anna were waiting day by day in the temple for the prophecy of Malachi to be fulfilled: 'The Lord whom you seek will suddenly come to his temple' (3:1). It is wonderful to be in the twilight years of life and yet still hopeful, still 'looking forward', still retaining a vibrant faith and a living hope.

Our God is the 'God of hope' (Romans 15:13), and those who believe in him never lose hope.

GENESIS 25:8–10 (NRSV, ABRIDGED)

The death of Abraham

Abraham breathed his last and died in a good old age, an old man and full of years, and was gathered to his people. His sons Isaac and Ishmael buried him in the cave of Machpelah, in… the field that Abraham purchased from the Hittites. There Abraham was buried, with his wife Sarah.

There is something strangely comforting about this brief account of the death of Abraham, father of the nation of Israel. Unlike Moses, he is given no magnificent epitaph, simply that he died 'in a good old age… full of years' (v. 8). This is, as it were, a 'family' death, involving the old man, full of years, his sons (who buried him) and his wife, Sarah, alongside whom he was buried. It's as though the story is complete and there is really no more to be said.

What it does emphasize is the role of family in our later years. Those who have never married, or not had children, may find in old age that they feel rather on their own. That is where friends, especially lifelong ones, can create a family for us, while nephews and nieces and their children and grandchildren can also create a very real sense of belonging to a family—and the people of Bible times would have recognized that to the full. For them, 'family' encompassed brothers and sisters, cousins and their families, and even the servants and slaves. They would not have recognized the idea of the 'lonely elderly' who are so much a feature of life today. Not only that, but to be old was to be honoured. Those who were 'full of years' were also seen as 'full of wisdom'—quite a contrast with the contemporary 'past it at forty' mentality!

We speak of God being 'with' us. How often, in practice, is that a matter of experiencing his presence in the familiar guise of family and friends?

EPHESIANS 5:15–16 (NRSV)

The value of time

**Be careful then how you live, not as unwise people but as
wise, making the most of the time, because the days are evil.**

At retirement, we tend to look back at our lives and ask ourselves
what we've made of them. It would be a rare person who felt that
they had used all the time God had given them to the full. Often
we are aware of years of wasted time. However, such feelings are
in fact futile: there is no rewind facility on the videotape of life.

It is far more profitable to look forward. How are we going
to spend whatever years the same God is going to give us in
retirement? I'm a bit sceptical of those who draw up a retirement
timetable: so much time in the garden, so much travelling, so
much time learning a new language or visiting old friends. Yet
plans (even abandoned plans) are better than drift, and there is
something very wasteful about what I would call a 'carpet-
slippers' retirement. There is time to live, and there are things to
do with it.

For the apostle, the call was not to misuse the most precious
gift we have—life itself. Human life is finite. We only have a
certain amount of time on earth to love and serve the giver. Paul
lists many unsavoury ways of wasting that time on what he calls
'the unfruitful works of darkness' (5:11). And that is their great
failure: they are 'unfruitful', they produce nothing of value or
beauty or usefulness.

His contrast is disarmingly simple: 'Try to find out what is
pleasing to the Lord' (5:10). I doubt if that means volunteering
for every vacant job at church. I suggest that it does mean
thought and prayer about how we are using the precious gift of
years of life after work.

Lord, may my twilight years be years of fruitfulness.

ECCLESIASTES 3:11–12, 14 (NRSV)

The 'proper' time

*[God] has made everything suitable for its time; moreover, he
has put a sense of past and future into [human] minds, yet
they cannot find out what God has done from the beginning
to the end. I know that there is nothing better for them than
to be happy and enjoy themselves as long as they live…
I know that whatever God does endures for ever; nothing can
be added to it, nor anything taken from it; God has done
this, so that all should stand in awe before him.*

These words follow the best-known lines in the book of
Ecclesiastes: 'For everything there is a season, and a time for every
matter under heaven' (3:1). The writer then moves on to these
philosophical musings, with their message that there is a 'proper'
time for things. Yet the mystery remains: only God knows what
lies ahead as well as what lies behind.

Time is one of the great mysteries of our existence. We
remember the past and we live in the present. For the future we
have two great gifts, faith and hope, but we have no knowledge of
what lies ahead. We cannot, in the writer's words, add anything to
what God does, nor can we take anything away from it.

'There is a time' for each part of our earthly lives. That is why, as
we stand on the threshold of any of life's junctions, we are able to
believe that the next part, like the previous one, is in God's hands.

For the person facing retirement, it surely means that fear is
an inappropriate response. This, too, is part of God's 'whole' and
every event in it is already known to him—moving home, or a
health condition, or the arrival of new grandchildren. Good and
bad, happy and sad, it can be 'proper' if seen as part of his
purposes of love.

Enjoyment is not self-indulgence but the will of a God who loves us.

JOHN 12:35–36a (NRSV)

Walking in the light

Jesus said to [the disciples], 'The light is with you for a little longer. Walk while you have the light, so that the darkness may not overtake you. If you walk in the darkness, you do not know where you are going. While you have the light, believe in the light, so that you may become children of light.'

The key word here is 'while'. The followers of Jesus were to make the most of that short period of time in which the light of the incarnation would shine in the world. Although the world would forget its brief day in the sun, the believers, making the most of the time they had, would themselves become 'children of light', carrying the light of Christ into the darkness of the world.

This explains why Jesus said, 'I am the light of the world' (John 8:12), but also, on a different occasion, 'You are the light of the world' (Matthew 5:14). Because the light of Christ had come, his followers could become reflectors of that light—always remembering that the light they bore was not their own, but his.

'While' is an important word in any language. It emphasizes that time is by its nature a passing phenomenon. We shall not always be as we are now, yet we are called to live in such a way now (while the 'light' shines) that when for a time it is taken away we may still be able to reflect it. We see this at work when a Christian who has sought to live in the light of Christ faces a dark or overshadowing experience—illness, bereavement, or deep disappointment. Into that darkness they carry the reflected light of Christ, gathered during the daylight hours, to light not only their own circumstances but the lives of those around them.

'Let your light shine before others, so that they may see'—not your sanctity, or courage, or even faith—'your good works and give glory to your Father in heaven.' (Matthew 5:16)

PSALM 139:1–3 (NRSV)

The open life

O Lord, you have searched me and known me. You know
when I sit down and when I rise up; you discern my thoughts
from far away. You search out my path and my lying down,
and are acquainted with all my ways.

Here is a theme we have already touched on, and yet one that, as we get older, makes more and more sense. Today's youngsters have an odd phrase, 'Stuff happens', which actually hides an enormous truth—that we can neither predict nor plan the future. Christians recognize that, though we can trust God for the future, only he knows what it holds. James expressed it in typically trenchant fashion in his epistle: 'Come now, you who say, "Today or tomorrow we will go to such and such a town and spend a year there…". Yet you do not even know what tomorrow will bring' (4:13–14). So much for those cherished plans for retirement! Mine took a nose-dive when my wife died a year or so after we had finally moved into the house we had chosen for our retirement.

The psalmist, in today's reading, puts it in more positive terms. God knows our actions in advance, reads our thoughts and charts our path through life. Rather than seeing this as a restrictive form of predestination, the psalmist is concerned with the benefits and blessings of such knowledge. If God knows, and we are in God's hands, then the open life is also the confident life. Events— 'stuff'—may take *us* by surprise, but not God.

This also means that there is no point in trying to hide things from God; even our secret thoughts are known to him. Again, that is reassuring rather than worrying. If he knows everything about us, and still shows us faithful love, what is there to fear from him?

God knows, God understands, God cares. That is our assurance for the future.

PSALM 130:5–6 (NRSV)

Learning patience

*I wait for the Lord, my soul waits, and in his word I hope;
my soul waits for the Lord more than those who watch for
the morning, more than those who watch for the morning.*

'Waiting' is a strange occupation, not popular with our time-driven world. 'I had to wait twenty minutes for a bus,' we fume. Or, 'You kept me waiting', as though that were a serious sin. Waiting was simply part of life in the society of biblical times. The farmer waited for the crops to ripen; the young woman waited for the baby to be born; the merchant waited for the camel train to arrive, not exactly to timetable! In the beautiful simile used here, during the night hours the watchmen sat on the city walls and waited for the first signs of dawn. In each case, waiting did not involve impatience, but assured hope. The crops would grow, the baby would be born, the merchants would pass by, and dawn would inevitably follow night. There is none of the impatience of modern life here; more, the understanding that, as we were reading earlier this week, 'for everything there is a season'.

As we grow older we tend to lose some of that youthful impatience. We have learnt that there are some things which simply cannot be hurried, indeed that there is a particular pleasure in anticipation fulfilled. Yet there is also a kind of 'senior impatience', a desperate feeling that if I don't do it now I may never do it at all. Perhaps because we know there is simply less time left for everything, what we perceive to be 'wasted' time is precisely that.

To 'wait for the Lord' is not a matter of foot-tapping impatience, but of simple trust. He has promised us good things and in his own time all will be revealed.

2 TIMOTHY 4:6–8 (NRSV, ABRIDGED)

The time of departure

As for me, I am already being poured out as a libation, and the time of my departure has come. I have fought the good fight, I have finished the race, I have kept the faith. From now on there is reserved for me the crown of righteousness, which the Lord, the righteous judge, will give me on that day, and… also to all who have longed for his appearing.

Time, as measured in human terms, has a fixed duration. We all know that the ultimate end is death, even though we probably try not to think about it too often. While modern medicine and a healthier lifestyle mean that the average person lives far beyond the biblical three score years and ten, even for Methuselah the day had to come. His 969 years end with the stark words, 'and he died' (see Genesis 5:27).

As Paul shows in today's passage, however, for the Christian that should be cause for neither fear nor regret. Death is not the end but the beginning—a departure for another shore.

Paul is able to look back on a life lived to the full: 'I have fought the good fight, I have finished the race, I have kept the faith' (v. 7). They are three wonderful claims to make at life's end, offering three different images of ultimate victory: the gladiator in the fight, the athlete in the race, and the confident believer. As the runner crosses the tape in first place, he or she doesn't, I imagine, regret that the race is over, but rejoices that it's been won.

So it is for the Christian. To die without regrets, looking back on days of God's blessing and mercy and ahead to the fulfilment of Christ's promises, is a privilege rather than a penalty.

As we get older, ambition gives way to memories. These are surely years to look back in thanksgiving, not because everything is 'over' but because everything is about to be transformed for good.

GENESIS 2:8, 18, 23–24 (NRSV)

Home, family, leisure

And the Lord God planted a garden in Eden, in the east; and there he put the man whom he had formed… Then the Lord God said, 'It is not good that the man should be alone; I will make him a helper as his partner.' … Then the man said, 'This at last is bone of my bones and flesh of my flesh; this one shall be called Woman, for out of Man this one was taken.' Therefore a man leaves his father and his mother and clings to his wife, and they become one flesh.

In this second account of the creation, the vast cosmic events of chapter 1 are distilled into an intensely human scene: the garden of delight, full of beauty, light, fruit and sweet scents; the man given the gentle task of tilling it and reaping its rich crops; and finally the arrival on the scene of man's 'other half', the woman to be his companion and partner. What more could anyone ask? Food, warmth, beauty, congenial work to do and wonderful, innocent love to complement it all.

This passage sets out in picture form the ingredients of the complete life. Satisfying work is one of them and so is the appreciation of the ordinary joys of life on earth. But supreme among them is the gift of companionship: 'it is not good that the man should be alone' (v. 18). There is a danger that in retirement we may feel deprived—perhaps one by one—of each of these ingredients. Our 'regular' work is over, we may even find that eyesight, hearing or smell are less responsive to our surroundings, and bereavement may deprive us of a beloved partner or friend.

All the more reason, then, to cherish our homes and families now, so that they are not strangers when we really need them.

During working life, home and family can sometimes be neglected. Retirement offers space and time to enjoy them afresh, as God intended.

PSALM 68:5–6a (NRSV)

God in the home

***Father of orphans and protector of widows is God in his holy
habitation. God gives the desolate a home to live in; he leads
out the prisoners to prosperity.***

God has made us gregarious, social creatures. While it is true that
sometimes, usually for short periods, most of us can value privacy,
to be deprived of all company for long seems unnatural. Even
monks and nuns live in 'communities'.

God cares for the orphan and the widow, the desolate and
lonely. That is why home is such an important part of normal life,
and why friends and family are so important to us. From my own
experience I can say that in the aftermath of bereavement they are
the most important human factors in recovery. This passage tells
us that they are a part of God's divine plan for the human race.

Retirement and advancing years (not always synonymous
nowadays!) refocus our lives on their importance. During working
life we probably see more of our immediate colleagues than we do
of husband, wife or children. The greater part of our waking life is
spent out of conscious contact with our nearest and dearest.

Now, however, the equation changes. Suddenly, we have 168
hours per week at home, even if 56 of them are spent asleep. We
may feel the need to rebuild entirely the relationships on which
our marriage or friendships are built. New tensions may emerge,
especially if one partner has more or less had the house to
themselves for 20 or 30 years. It's a moment for looking afresh at
God's place in the home and his priorities for his creatures in it.
If he puts us together, as part of his loving purpose, then
presumably he expects us to find that a blessing, not a burden.

*Retirement may be the moment not for a final winding down, but for a
completely new and fresh look at our priorities, goals and relationships.*

2 THESSALONIANS 3:11–13 (NRSV)

Avoiding idleness

For we hear that some of you are living in idleness, mere busybodies, not doing any work. Now such persons we command and exhort in the Lord Jesus Christ to do their work quietly and to earn their own living. Brothers and sisters, do not be weary in doing what is right.

Retirement, certainly in its early years, is not an opportunity to do nothing, but to do something new and different. The Christians at Thessalonica were so sure that the second coming of the Lord Jesus was imminent that some of them had decided there was no point in doing work or earning a living—after all, they would soon be in the kingdom of heaven, where presumably there are no chores!

Some of us have a certain penchant for doing nothing, and retirement might seem to be a splendid opportunity to indulge it. Hours and days beckon, and so does the armchair and the television. All quite harmless, of course, but a waste of precious hours if they fill up all our days. Many a newly retired person has, quite understandably, spent the first few months in some such blissful state of inertia, only to find that there is no better recipe for inducing premature senility! In the end, we look to fill the time newly available rather more productively and creatively, and in doing so keep ourselves young, alert and interesting.

How we make the most of this new time is a personal decision. It is perhaps too easy simply to be drawn into taking on roles in church, charity or club—though many such bodies depend on the energy of the newly retired to survive. On the other hand, if we have gifts and experience—and even a little wisdom accumulated over the years—now is emphatically the time to put it to good use.

Idleness is wasted time, frenetic activity is distorted time, but the life newly offered to God is redeemed time.

MATTHEW 6:26–29 (NRSV)

Time to stand and stare

Look at the birds of the air; they neither sow nor reap nor gather into barns, and yet your heavenly Father feeds them. Are you not of more value than they? And can any of you by worrying add a single hour to your span of life? And why do you worry about clothing? Consider the lilies of the field, how they grow; they neither toil nor spin, yet I tell you, even Solomon in all his glory was not clothed like one of these.

'I never noticed'—I have lost count of the number of times I have said that, though less frequently in the gentler years of retirement. Much of working life is so pressurized that our eyes are firmly fixed on 'goals'. Where am I due next? Why is this train so slow? Can I get this report completed during the flight? Time to stand and stare, look and listen: that can be relegated to 'any other business'.

Jesus tells his hearers, the people of the kingdom, to 'look at' and 'consider' not programmes, propositions or doctrines, but birds and flowers. Is this an invitation to fly off with the fairies? On the contrary, the result of their looking and considering will be the justice and righteousness of God's kingdom (see 6:33) or, more simply, a complete readjustment of their priorities of life (see 6:30–32). To rush through life with eyes blinkered by our limited objectives is to miss the splendour and truth of the whole picture.

'I never noticed!' In the hectic rush, I had no time and space to see what really mattered, who really loved me, what the true values of life are. Well, at least retirement should offer us space to put that right, even if somewhat belatedly. Take a look at the birds, study the flowers, and remind yourself that 'you are of more value than many sparrows' (Matthew 10:31).

'A poor life this if, full of care, we have no time to stand and stare.'
(W.H. Davies)

1 TIMOTHY 5:8–10 (NRSV)

The responsibilities of age

Whoever does not provide for relatives, and especially for family members, has denied the faith and is worse than an unbeliever. Let a widow be put on the list if she is not less than sixty years old and has been married only once; she must be well attested for her good works, as one who has brought up children, shown hospitality, washed the saints' feet, helped the afflicted, and devoted herself to doing good in every way.

This is another fascinating glimpse into the life of the early Christian Church. There were no state pension schemes, no social services and no retirement homes. There was, however, a general acceptance that the Church had a responsibility to some of its older members, and that each Christian family had the duty of caring for its own dependants.

The passage also reminds us that advancing years carry responsibilities. The retired person may be tempted to feel that what they have earned during working life is their own, to be spent as they wish. The idea of a worldwide tour, which leaves very little in the bank but a tan on the face and a full photograph album, can be very appealing! Before it is embarked on, however, these words might be pondered. The money is ours, and both legally and morally we have a right to spend it, but would it be irresponsible to blow the lot if there are family members who need care?

For the person approaching retirement this cuts both ways, of course. We may find that we are the ones who need support from family (and even, one would like to think, the church). Or we may be the ones still in a position to offer support to those further along the journey, finding in later years that savings have all but gone and life has suddenly become much less comfortable.

Either to give or to accept another's support requires grace.

PSALM 1:1–3 (NRSV)

The life that does not wither

Happy are those who do not follow the advice of the wicked, or take the path that sinners tread, or sit in the seat of scoffers; but their delight is in the law of the Lord, and on his law they meditate day and night. They are like trees planted by streams of water, which yield their fruit in its season, and their leaves do not wither. In all that they do, they prosper.

One could call these verses 'the secret of a serene life', and there's just a hint that it applies especially to those who are older ('whose leaves do not wither', v. 3). I don't think there's much evidence that retired people are notably more 'wicked' than others, but 'scoffing' is not unknown, especially of the kind that can see little good in the present and constantly harks back to the imagined 'good old days'.

In any case, there can be little doubt that the serene life is the best alternative to aged discontent. Here, the psalmist argues that it is the 'good' life that knows serenity—'good' in the sense that it is shaped by God's precepts and nourished by the springs of living water. The image of trees is interesting, too: they take a very long time to grow, absorb an enormous amount of water, and produce leaves in abundance when they are suitably fed. Many of them also produce fruit. The trees in this image are actually planted by the riverside, so the source of nourishment is readily at hand.

Here is a picture of contented retirement: not idleness, but not frantic activity either; not a scornful rejection of the present or a constant dwelling on the past, but a glad and positive engagement with both; not a stealthy step or two away from God and his truth, but a fresh embracing of them. In my experience, those whose later years are lived like that live them to the full.

In that 'good life' of which the psalmist speaks, an essential element is a balance between rest and activity, home and travel, work and worship.

MONDAY

HEBREWS 13:5–6, 8 (NRSV)

A firm foundation

Keep your lives free from the love of money, and be content with what you have; for he has said, 'I will never leave you or forsake you.' So we can say with confidence, 'The Lord is my helper; I will not be afraid. What can anyone do to me?' … Jesus Christ is the same yesterday and today and for ever.

I knew an elderly man some years ago whose main, if not only, topic of conversation was money. Even on first acquaintance, he would ask people of his own age what kind of investments they had and how they were doing—to be topped, of course, by a detailed account of his own financial transactions. Certainly in retirement financial insecurity can be a besetting anxiety, but to 'be content' is presumably to live happily with what we have, and not worry too much about what others have got—or even what we used to have.

The lasting security of all Christians, young and old, is spelt out in this passage: the Lord will never leave us or forsake us. The writer of Hebrews draws the logical deduction from this. If the Lord is truly our helper, what can any human being do to harm us? There is therefore nothing to fear, in the present or for the future.

One question remains, of course. God made that promise long, long ago, to people very different from ourselves. Can we be sure that it is still effective? Again, the answer is categorical: 'Jesus Christ is the same yesterday and today and for ever' (v. 8). In a rapidly changing world we may feel that very little is the same even as it was ten years ago. Yet Christ does not and cannot change, because he is divine, and what is divine is not subject to change.

'Change and decay in all around I see'—so wrote H.F. Lyte in his great hymn 'Abide with me', but 'change' and 'decay' are not synonymous! Of course, life changes, and so does our situation. The Christian faith is not in an unchanging scene, but in an unchanging God.

PSALM 91:1–2 (NRSV)

A safe stronghold

You who live in the shelter of the Most High, who abide in the shadow of the Almighty, will say to the Lord, 'My refuge and my fortress; my God, in whom I trust.'

'Refuges' and 'fortresses' were highly significant to the people of the ancient world. A place of safety to spend the night, secure from predatory animals or people, was a necessity, not a luxury. Each tribal area or kingdom needed its fortress, its 'high tower', where the population could flee when menaced by an invading enemy. The equivalent for us would probably be fall-out shelters or bomb-proof office blocks. The people of ancient Israel were called by the psalmist to think of God as their shelter, their refuge and their fortress—the place of safety and protection in time of danger.

In fact, of course, our lives are as perilous as theirs, though in different ways. For most of us, advancing years—yes, even the arrival of retirement—increase our awareness that life is insecure. The young tend to live as though they are immortal. It would not be normal for a healthy 20- or 30-year-old to be haunted by thoughts of illness, incapacity or death. As the years pass, however, we can hardly avoid the inevitable awareness of our own human frailty and of the fact that life itself moves towards its eternal destination with remorseless tread. Again, I don't mean that the over-60s spend sleepless nights worrying about such things, but that they do worm into our mental agenda.

As for the Israelites in their hamlets and villages, so for us in our comfortable centrally heated homes: security is not to be found in money, bricks and mortar or even people. Our refuge is the Almighty; we live 'in the shelter of the Most High' (v. 1).

When the storm blows, it is well to know where to find a safe place.

PSALM 91:3–6 (NRSV)

Antidote to fears

For he will deliver you from the snare of the fowler and from the deadly pestilence; he will cover you with his pinions, and under his wings you will find refuge; his faithfulness is a shield and buckler. You will not fear the terror of the night, or the arrow that flies by day, or the pestilence that stalks in darkness, or the destruction that wastes at noonday.

We can have irrational fears at any age, and whenever they arise, they are generally worse than rational ones, because there is simply no answer to them. I knew a woman who was paralysed with fear every time her adult son flew to the USA on business (which was, roughly speaking, monthly). It was no use telling her that planes fly back and forth across the Atlantic all day long without crashing, or that she was in more danger walking to the post office for her pension. Fear ate away at her mind, fuelled by imagination—the 'just supposing' kind of anxiety that knows no antidote.

Whenever life feels less secure or we go through a period of change—however welcome in other ways—such fears may come. When they do, the believer has recourse to a powerful antidote, though its application does require an act of faith. The psalmist expresses it here in beautiful poetry. Whether it be the physical danger of attack by day, or the nameless dread that may haunt us in a dream at night, or an epidemic that's hitting the headlines ('the pestilence') or even the 'destruction' of natural disaster, God will cover his children with his 'wings', drawing them into a place of divine shelter. This is no guarantee of immunity. It is much more: it is a promise of his presence whatever and whoever menaces us.

On the whole, when we are anxious it is not arguments or logic that we seek, but a sympathetic ear and a shoulder to rest on. Here the promise is of wings and pinions to hide under!

MATTHEW 6:31–34 (NRSV, ABRIDGED)

The future is safe

'Therefore do not worry, saying, "What will we eat?" or "What will we drink?" or "What will we wear?" For… your heavenly Father knows that you need all these things. But strive first for the kingdom of God and his righteousness, and all these things will be given to you as well. So do not worry about tomorrow, for tomorrow will bring worries of its own. Today's trouble is enough for today.'

Today's reading may be similar to yesterday's, but it is in several respects 'closer to home' for the retired person. One feature of retirement is a change in pattern of income—from payslip to pension, in most cases. In fact, many people nowadays actually feel better off retired. The mortgage has been paid off, children are supporting themselves, it may be possible to 'downsize' where housing is concerned and bank the difference. Yet anxiety can feature strongly in the later stages of life, not simply or even mainly about money but about health, and the health of those close to us.

Jesus actually says 'don't worry about tomorrow', but it is almost always 'tomorrow' that we do worry about. If we analyse our fears, they are usually about things that actually haven't happened yet. With stern practicality Jesus points out that we'll find another set of things to worry about when tomorrow becomes today!

His answer, as so often, is to get our priorities right, to strive first to live our lives under the gracious and just rule of a loving God— and then to leave the consequences to him. To do that will be much more satisfying than feeding our fears. All that we need, all the reassurance we seek, will be added by the Lord as a kind of bonus.

Jesus the realist does not suggest that troubles will not come, but he puts them into perspective. If God is in charge, not simply eternally but daily, then 'your wants shall be his care' (Nahum Tate & Nicholas Brady).

PSALM 121:5–8 (NRSV)

The life watched over

The Lord is your keeper; the Lord is your shade at your right hand. The sun shall not strike you by day, nor the moon by night. The Lord will keep you from all evil; he will keep your life. The Lord will keep your going out and your coming in from this time on and for evermore.

This week we have been thinking of the foundations of faith, which are an unchanging God who remains with us 'through all the changing scenes of life'. Today, we are invited to consider the 'life watched over'. The picture is one of gentle but ceaseless supervision of our lives—a bit like having a constantly present but endlessly caring security guard! And that keeper is the Lord himself, who watches over each step that we take, going out or coming in.

The heat of the sun is not the greatest worry for northern Europeans for most of the year, but in the ancient Middle East it must have been a constant trial. Hence, 'the Lord is your shade' (v. 5) by day. The moon is a bit different! It's not its heat but its supposed effect on people's behaviour that creates anxiety. (This used to be called 'lunacy'—eccentric behaviour prompted by lunar movements.) Here, too, the Lord is our shade.

The 'going out' and the 'coming in' probably refer to the way city and town dwellers left in the morning, going out through the gates in the wall for their day's work in the fields, and then returned in the evening. Outside the walls they were vulnerable to attack by robbers or wild animals, so 'going out and coming in' were important moments in the day's routine. In both cases the Lord was 'watching over' them.

Most of us would probably rather not be watched over in a 'Big Brother' sense, but the Lord's care for us is not dictatorial or intrusive. We are permanently under the observation of a loving eye.

Everything new!

And I heard a loud voice from the throne saying, 'See, the home of God is among mortals. He will dwell with them; they will be his peoples, and God himself will be with them; he will wipe every tear from their eyes. Death will be no more; mourning and crying and pain will be no more, for the first things have passed away.' And the one who was seated on the throne said, 'See, I am making all things new.'

I was enthusing over the vintage car, a 1930 Bentley, when the owner rather spoilt things. Yes, it was the 1930 model, and in that sense it was well over 70 years old, but the only part in the present vehicle which had left the factory all those years ago was the hooter. Everything else had been replaced. Many people in later years are having a similar experience. I have a completely new lens in my right eye. I have friends with new hips, new knees, a new kidney—and there are also, of course, hundreds of people walking around with new hearts. We are deeply into replacement medicine, but no matter how many new bits we put in, we are still the 1932 or 1935 or 1944 model!

Here God's promise is to make 'everything' new—our bodies, yes, in the resurrection; but also the very environment in which we exist. It's hard to imagine life without tears, mourning, pain or death, yet this is the picture we are offered of life in the 'new Jerusalem', the city of God, whose lights shine in the distance to welcome the earthly pilgrim as journey's end is reached. Here is the total transformation of human existence, the reversal of the Fall, the blessing long promised. Here 'the home of God is among mortals' (v. 3). We have not 'gone' to heaven; heaven has 'come' to us!

Often the best part of the journey comes after the end of it.

Bible reading notes from BRF

If you have found this booklet helpful and would like to continue reading the Bible regularly, you may like to explore BRF's three series of Bible reading notes.

NEW DAYLIGHT

New Daylight offers a devotional approach to reading the Bible. Each issue covers four months of daily Bible readings and reflection from a regular team of contributors (including David Winter), who represent a stimulating mix of church backgrounds. Each day's reading provides a Bible passage (text included), comment and prayer or thought for reflection. In *New Daylight* the Sundays and special festivals from the church calendar are noted on the relevant days, to help you appreciate the riches of the Christian year.

DAY BY DAY WITH GOD

Day by Day with God (published jointly with Christina Press) is written especially for women, with a regular team of contributors. Each four-monthly issue offers daily Bible readings, with key verses printed out, helpful comment, a prayer or reflection for the day ahead, and suggestions for further reading.

GUIDELINES

Guidelines is a unique Bible reading resource that offers four months of in-depth study written by leading scholars. Contributors are drawn from around the world, as well as the UK, and they represent a thought-provoking breadth of Christian tradition. *Guidelines* is written in weekly units consisting of six sections plus an introduction and a final section of points for thought and prayer.

If you would like to subscribe to one or more of these sets of Bible reading notes, please use the order form overleaf

SUBSCRIPTIONS

❏ I would like to give a gift subscription (please complete both
   name and address sections below)
❏ I would like to take out a subscription myself (complete name
   and address details only once)

This completed coupon should be sent with appropriate payment to BRF.
Alternatively, please write to us quoting your name, address, the subscription
you would like for either yourself or a friend (with their name and address),
the start date and credit card number, expiry date and signature if paying by
credit card.

Gift subscription name _____

Gift subscription address_____

_____

_____Postcode _____

Please send beginning with the January / May / September issue:
(delete as applicable)

(please tick box)	UK	SURFACE	AIR MAIL
NEW DAYLIGHT	❏ £11.70	❏ £13.05	❏ £15.30
GUIDELINES	❏ £11.70	❏ £13.05	❏ £15.30
DAY BY DAY WITH GOD	❏ £12.45	❏ £13.80	❏ £16.05

Please complete the payment details below and send your coupon,
with appropriate payment to: **BRF, First Floor, Elsfield Hall, 15–17
Elsfield Way, Oxford OX2 8FG.**

Your name _____

Your address _____

_____

_____Postcode _____

Total enclosed £ _____ (cheques made payable to 'BRF')

Payment: cheque ❏ postal order ❏ Visa ❏ Mastercard ❏ Switch ❏

Card number: ☐☐☐☐☐☐☐☐☐☐☐☐☐☐☐☐☐☐☐☐

Expiry date of card: ☐☐☐☐ Issue number (Switch): ☐☐☐☐

Signature (essential if paying by credit/Switch card)

❏ Please do not send me further information about BRF publications.

BRF resources are available from your local Christian bookshop. BRF is a Registered Charity